NOVELLO HANDEL EDITION

General Editor: Watkins Shaw

As Pants the Hart

Anthem 6B, HWV 251^C, Version A & B
for SAATBB (or SATB) soli, SATB chorus & orchestra

Words from Psalm 42

Edited by Donald Burrows

vocal score

Order No: NOV 070488

NOVELLO PUBLISHING LIMITED

PREFACE

Handel seems to have had a particular liking for *As Pants the Hart*, for he produced several settings of the text. Two versions (Anthems 6C and 6D)[1] are 'verse' anthems without orchestral accompaniment: they were composed for the Chapel Royal and the earlier version is almost certainly Handel's first piece of English church music, composed *c*1712. Anthem 6A is the 'Chandos' version, produced in 1717 for the singers and instrumentalists employed by James Brydges at Edgware. Anthem 6B, presented here in Handel's two versions, has orchestral accompaniment and constitutes the composer's latest settings of the text. The words, a free mixture of verses from Psalm 42 as translated in the Authorised Version of the Bible and the *Book of Common Prayer*, remained fundamentally the same through each of Handel's versions; in origin the arrangement of the text may owe something to that of an anthem (now lost) composed by Dr John Arbuthnot, one of the Physicians to Queen Anne and a close friend of Handel during his early years in London. Handel's various versions exhibit a fascinating mixture of new composition with adaptation and recomposition of previous material: only the music of the first vocal movement remained relatively permanent through all the versions. Anthem 6B, as well as including some completely fresh material, also incorporates some compositional improvements that had occurred to Handel in the course of developing his previous versions.

Handel's two versions presented here were performed under different circumstances, and the differences between them are the consequence of the composer's desire to match the music to the occasion and the forces available. The first version was composed *c*1722 for a service in the Chapel Royal, St James's Palace. The Chapel is fairly small, and the group of performers (consisting of Boys and Gentlemen of the Chapel Royal, string players from the King's Musicians and a few additional instrumentalists) was small, perhaps less than thirty performers in all. The second version was performed at the King's Theatre, Haymarket, as the opening item of Handel's benefit concert in March 1738, entitled simply 'An Oratorio'. Later items in the programme included Italian arias and large-scale choruses derived from *Deborah* and the Coronation Anthems, from which it appears that Handel had at his disposal some of the leading members of his current opera company and also the additional singers (including some from the Chapel Royal) that constituted his chorus for oratorio performances. Therefore the second version, in addition to being rather more extended, was prepared for a larger and more heterogeneous group of performers. This is the first edition of the anthem to distinguish clearly between the musical contents of the two versions.

VERSION 1: (Chapel Royal, 1722). For this version the shorter (Version A) endings to No. 1 and No. 7 should be followed, No. 4A performed and No. 4B omitted.

VERSION 2: (An Oratorio, 1738). For this version the longer (Version B) endings to No. 1 and No. 7 should be followed, and No. 4B performed in place of No. 4A.

Soloists

The principal solo work falls to one each of alto, tenor and bass voices. Only in No. 2 are further soloists required. If the anthem is performed by an expert small choir, many of whose members are accustomed to act as soloists, then Handel's original scheme for No. 2 presents no problems. With a larger choral society this arrangement may not be possible or may be regarded as wasteful if a second alto and a second bass are not required elsewhere in the programme. In such a case, the solo music in No. 2 may be taken by the conventional four SATB soloists following the alternative plan suggested editorially next to the vocal lines.

In the Chapel Royal version Handel's soloists in No. 2 were Mr Hughs (Francis Hughes)(*A1*), Mr (Thomas) Bell (*A2*), Mr Getting (Thomas Gethin) (*T*), Mr Whely (Samuel Weely)(*B1*), Mr (Thomas) Baker (*B2*), and an unnamed treble. All of the subsequent alto solos were taken by Hughes, and Bell sang the tenor-clef solo in No. 6. Weely sang the bass solo in No. 4A, and Baker the solo at the start of No. 7: a similar division might be followed if two bass soloists are available. Singers are also named at the start of No. 5 in Handel's autograph, but as leading voices in the chorus parts rather than as soloists. Handel's intentions over the solo-chorus transitions in No. 2 are unclear in three places:

> Bar 18 Alto 1. It appears that Handel wrote 'Chorus' and then smudged the word out.
> Bar 19 Bass 1, Bass 2. No directions in voice parts, but 'Chorus' next to *bc*.
> Bar 37 Bass 1. No directions.

It may have been the case that Handel was uncertain whether his 'chorus' would include any voices other than his named soloists at this stage, but the appearances of 'Solo' against Alto 1 at bar 28 and against Bass 1 at bar 31 suggest otherwise, so chorus entries have been interpreted editorially. It is clear nevertheless that Handel's soloists also sang through the relevant chorus lines throughout the anthem.

The identities of the soloists in Handel's 1738 performance of the anthem are not known. Handel's opera cast from the period contained no English singers, and the alto-range soloists were contraltos rather than *castrati*. The solo music in the anthem may have been taken either by opera soloists or by members of the chorus.

iii

Instrumentation – oboes and violins

Handel's Chapel Royal version was performed by a single oboe and a small group of strings, and Nos. 1 and 3 exploit the contrast between the oboe soloist and the string ensemble. At the beginning of No. 6 Handel labelled the upper instrumental staves simply 'H' and 'V': this was interpreted in an authoritative early copy (Source **B**, below) as 'Hautb.' and 'Violin solo'. The allocation of most of the movement to a solo violin may perhaps be justified by Handel's 'tutti' at bar 92 next to the Violin 1 stave. His practice in 1738 is less easy to determine. The oboe parts in No. 1 (bars 24 – 32), No. 3, and No. 6 (bars 1 – 83) may have been taken by a soloist, matched by a solo violin in No. 6. Alternatively Handel may have preferred a more robust interpretation for his theatre performance, doubling the oboe part throughout with two players and maintaining the full body of strings: the Second Oboe part from Source **L**, while not deriving directly from Handel's performance, suggests that such a treatment was regarded as normal by a copyist from the 'Smith circle'. When performing Version 2 conductors may therefore choose the interpretation most suitable to their own circumstances with regard to the violin part in No. 6 and the oboe parts in those movements that were originally composed for a single oboe. The Oboe 2 part supplied with the hire material for this edition is a 'full' part with solo indications for use at discretion.

Instrumentation – the bass line

Against the bass line of No. 3 Handel wrote 'Organo, Violoncello, e Contrabassi'. This may be a precise statement of his forces in 1722 for Version 1, when the King's Musicians may only have provided a single 'cello while two double basses were named in the Lord Chamberlain's papers as additional performers. No bassoon is mentioned in Handel's score, and the instrument's participation in Version 1 is uncertain. Handel's additional music for 1738 assumes two oboes and, although bassoons are not specifically mentioned, we can assume that at least two contributed to the bass line. A bassoon part, derived editorially from the basso continuo line, is available for use *ad libitum* with either version, and may be doubled in the choruses in Version 2.

The Continuo group

Handel's 'solo' and 'tutti' markings at various points in the *basso continuo* line reflect the texture of the orchestral accompaniments above and the alternations of soloists and chorus. In general, passages marked 'solo' can appropriately be dealt with by lightening the bass line to a single 'cello, with

keyboard continuo. The 'solo' passages in No. 3 are also included in the *ad libitum* bassoon part, for optional use in accompanying the oboe solos.

The organ is specified by Handel as the chord-playing continuo instrument in Version 1. For Version 2 Handel may well have followed theatrical practice by using the harpsichord as the principal keyboard instrument, with organ (or organs) supporting the choruses. See also source **E**, below.

Sources

1. PRINCIPAL SOURCE

A London, British Library (Reference Division), RM 20.g.1. Handel's autograph of Version 1, with his pencilled amendments for Version 2. A copy of No. 4^B in the hand of J.C. Smith the elder is inserted, cancelling No. 4^A: the reason for its inclusion is that this MS also apparently served as a performance score in 1738 and Handel's autograph of No. 4^B had been written on paper of a different format. Some *tempo* indications elsewhere in the MS are in Smith's hand, as detailed below.

2. PRIMARY SOURCE FOR VERSION 1

B London, British Library (Reference Division), Add. MS 31557, ff. 3 – 31. Transcript, *c*1722, in the hand of Smith senior. Bound with a copy of Anthem 6A: a title page of early origin erroneously describes the contents as 'Two Anthem's Composed for his Grace the Duke of Shandous by G.F.Handel Esquire 1719'. Later annotations draw attention to various additions to the score of Anthem 6B as being in Handel's hand: all but two of these can be dismissed. The 'Largo' at the start of No. 2 appears to be Handel's, as also the notes added to the *bc* part at No. 6 bars 79, 81, 83 replacing whole-bar rests. The added notes in No. 6, placed in brackets in this edition, were not copied into source **A** and do not appear in any other source. Presumably they reflect an afterthought relating to the 1722 performance, and were not repeated in 1738.

This source establishes beyond doubt the precise form of Version 1, and Handel's annotations suggest that it was a conducting score prepared for the Chapel Royal performance. With the possible exception of the first state of source **J**, no other secondary copy reflects the state of the anthem before the 1738 additions were inserted.

3. PRIMARY SOURCES FOR VERSION 2

C Printed word-book entitled 'An Oratorio. As it is Perform'd at the King's Theatre in the Hay-Market. Compos'd by Mr. Handel' (Watts, London, 1738). This gives, on pp. 4 – 5, the text of the anthem as performed in Version 2. The opening words of No. 5 appear as 'In the Voice

iv

of Praise, of Thanksgiving'. Copy in the Rowe Library, King's College, Cambridge.

D British Library, Add. MS 30308, ff. 27 – 28. Handel's autograph of No. 4^B, composed in 1738. Ends with a cue to No. 5. Includes incidental reference to two oboes in scoring.

E Cambridge, Fitzwilliam Museum, Music MS 265, pp. 53 – 55, 61. Fragmentary performance part for *An Oratorio*, 1738, in the hand of Smith senior. Begins at No. 7 bar 40, giving the ending for Version B. 5 bars in full score, followed by figured bass for remainder of movement. Presumably prepared to Handel's verbal directions, with reference to a vertical cue-line in pencil at No. 7 bar 40 in source **A**. Format and layout at the opening suggest that the MS was placed at the end of source **A** for practical use in 1738, from which we might infer that Handel directed the anthem on that occasion from the harpsichord. This source discloses that the 'Alleluja', composed originally in $\frac{2}{4}$ metre (in source **G**), was re-barred into common time for the anthem and followed No. 7 bar 39 without any change of tempo.

F British Library, RM 20.d.8, ff. 31 – 33. Handel's autograph of No. 1 (Version B ending) bars 54 – 129, taken from the 'Chandos' anthem *In the Lord put I my trust*.

G British Library, RM 20.h.1, ff.26 – 28v. Handel's autograph of No. 7 (Version B ending) bars 40½ – 108, taken from the oratorio *Athalia*.

H Hamburg, Staats- und Universitätsbibliothek, MS MC/264, ff.46*bis* (following f.50), 51 – 54. Copy of source **G** in the hand of Smith senior, in the conducting score of *Athalia*. From markings in the next movement it is apparent that this score was used for the preparation of some material for the 1738 *Oratorio*: the pencilled cue-marks at the beginning of the 'Alleluja' and an additional note in the viola part are, however, related to the 1735 revival of *Athalia* and not to the 1738 *Oratorio*.

4. SECONDARY SOURCE MATERIAL

J Durham, Cathedral Library, MS E26(5). Score in the hand of Larsen's copyist S4, now fragmentary and containing only No. 1 bars 18 – 52 and No. 2 bars 1 – 3. Probably copied *c*1735 for Oxford musicians. Pencilled cue in the hand of Richard Fawcett for the 1738 addition to No. 1.

K British Library, Egerton MS 2911, ff.1 – 21v. 'Granville Collection' score copied *c*1740 by copyist Larsen S1. Version 1, but with No. 4^B instead of No. 4^A. The copyist apparently made some guesses as to Handel's intentions when he labelled instrumental staves, assigning one bass line in No. 5 to bassoons and interpreting the opening treble lines of No. 6 as solos for oboe and violin.

L Chicago, Joseph Regenstein Library, University of Chicago, MS 437, vols. 2, 3, 5, 7, 12, 14, 16, 18, 20, 22. 'Aylesford' Collection instrumental and vocal parts in the hand of copyist S2, including the anthem, presumably derived from a score now lost, and in a hybrid form, which probably reflects a copyist's attempt to understand **A** as it stood after the 1738 amendments. No. 1 has the ending for Version 1, but followed by the second movement of the Sinfonia to Anthem 6A transposed to D minor: it seems most likely that the copyist, coming upon Handel's pencilled cue for the *allegro* movement in **A**, could not find the correct movement and so substituted one that seemed appropriate. No. 4^A and No. 7 appear as in Version 1, but No. 4^B is also inserted as an alternative. The two instrumental bass parts are designated 'Organo & Contrabasso' and 'Violoncello & Bassone' and this arrangement is maintained throughout, the second part even including music in No. 2 that Handel specifically allocated to double bass. In No. 6 the copyist took the opposite line from the copyist of source **K** and interpreted the opening violin and oboe parts as 'tutti'. Although interesting as an example of how this particular copyist extracted orchestral parts from a score in the mid-1740s, there is nothing to suggest that his interpretations should be regarded as finally authoritative.

M British Library, RM 19.a.1, ff.148 – 150. Score of No.4^B in a miscellaneous 'Aylesford' volume, in the hand of S2. Presumably complementing the parts for this movement inserted into source **L**.

N Hamburg, Staats- und Universitätsbibliothek, MS MC/261a, Vol II, ff.8 – 11. Score of No. 2, inserted into a conducting score of *Esther* for performances under J.C.Smith junior in 1767 – 8. Copyist S5.

O Hamburg, Staats- und Universitätsbibliothek, MS MA/177, 'Vol.VI'. Score, one volume from a collection apparently assembled by Oxford musicians associated with William Hayes in the late 1760s. Scribe unidentified. No. 1 appears as Version 1, but Version 2 is represented by No. 4^B and by the longer ending to No. 7. This copy was marked up by Friedrich Chrysander as the copy-text from which the printer prepared the first printed edition of the anthem in 1871 (*Händelgesellschaft*, Vol.34, pp.239 – 276).

P British Library, RM 19.g.1, Vol.1, ff.1 – 29v. Score, 'Smith Collection' *c*1770, in the hand of copyist S11. Contents similar to source **L** but with No. 4^B only in place of No. 4^A.

Q Rutgers University Library, New Brunswick, Department of Special Collections, MS M2038. H14A5, Vol. 6(1), pp.1 – 99. Score, copied *c*1770 by 'Picker "A"'[2]. Formerly part of the collection of Sir Watkin Williams Wynn and referred to by Charles Burney in *An Account of the Musical Performances . . . in Commemoration of Handel* (1785). Contents as for source **P**.

R Oxford, Christ Church, MSS 69, 72. Parts for Canto and Tenor voices in the hands of Richard Goodson junior (d.1741) and Richard Fawcett. Probably copied c1740 for performances in Oxford. Derived from the score of which source **J** remains, with 1738 additions.

S Durham, Cathedral Library, MS E26. Violino Primo Concertino part for the 1738 version in the hand of Richard Fawcett. Apparently connected with source **R**, but derived from a different source and probably of rather later date.

Sources **N** – **Q** and **S** share a number of corrupt readings, suggesting that they derived from a common secondary source that cannot now be identified.

Although not of immediate relevance to the preparation of this edition, one further source is of interest on account of its early date. An arrangement of the anthem, transposed to C minor and with organ accompaniment, appears in the eighteenth-century choir books at Durham Cathedral. This arrangement includes some music from Version 2 and it is apparent from the copying dates in MS B 26 that the music was prepared before Michaelmas 1738.

Editorial Procedure and Commentary

Handel's autographs in sources **A**, **D**, **F** and **G** have been treated as the prime source for readings of notes and textual underlay, with reference to the other principal sources as necessary for clarification. Some tempo indications are derived from source **B**, as detailed below. The overall scheme of the anthem's two versions is based on source **B** for Version 1, and on the combined evidence of sources **A**, **C** and **E** for Version 2. The interpretation of Handel's adaptations to **A** in 1738 can be summarised thus:

No.1 Handel deleted bars 50 – 52 of Version A and wrote the alternative ending in pencil (now very faded). He gave a two-bar cue for the 'Chandos' anthem movement, marked 'Fuga, allegro'. As composed in source **F** this movement was scored for an ensemble with a single oboe and no violas. It seems a reasonable assumption that in 1738 the oboe part was doubled by Oboe 2. For the viola I have provided editorially a part based on the arrangement of the movement in Walsh's edition of the Concerto Op. 3 No. 5, published in 1734, with the viola mainly doubling the bass part an octave higher.

No.4♭ Source **D** ends with a cue that suggests that this movement runs into No. 5 without any change of speed. In **A**, Smith's tempo 'allegro' for No. 5 has been deleted in pencil: I take this to mean that the

'allegro' only applies to Version 1 and that the beginning of No. 5 should follow No. 4♭ without a break, *l'istesso tempo* (actually 'andante') in Version 2.

No.7 Source **E** has been taken as the copy-text for the linking bars 40 – 41, and as a guide to the barring of the rest of the movement.

Numbering of movements is editorial. C clefs for soprano, alto, and tenor voices are transcribed in the G clef, and the time-signature **c** rendered as $\frac{4}{4}$. Horizontal square brackets are editorial marks of re-grouping in triple time. Suggestions for rhythmic alteration are shown above the stave. Small size notation is an editorial expansion of the composer's text, mainly with regard to continuo realisation. Material in square brackets is editorial. Cancelling accidentals, when not provided by the composer, have been supplied editorially in the modern convention without typographical distinction, likewise a few cautionary accidentals. In only one place (No. 1 bar 15, beat 3) is Handel not entirely explicit in his intentions concerning accidentals: the B natural has been supplied here from Handel's copy of a virtually identical bar in *The Anthem on the Peace* (British Library, RM 20.g.6, f.25v). Editorial slurs and ties are marked by a dash, thus: ⌢.

The following points call for individual comment. In what follows, (*Sm*) identifies items in the handwriting of J.C.Smith senior: his tempo indications were presumably added at Handel's direction, and some of them may have been derived from comparable movements in the 'verse' Anthem 6D (British Library, RM 20.g.10).

No. 1 Title 'Sinfonia', taken from **B** (*Sm*), not present in **A**.

Bars 2, 4, 6 Violins. The similar opening to 'Chandos' Anthem 6A has trills to beat 1, but Handel did not repeat the trills here. They appear in none of the early sources, but occur in the later MSS of the **N** – **Q**, **S** group, presumably as the result of editorial activity in comparison with Anthem 6A. While it is not impossible that the omission of the trills in Anthem 6B (and in the derived movement for the *Anthem on the Peace*) was merely an oversight on Handel's part, it is equally likely that the omission was deliberate and related to differences in the circumstances of performance.

No. 2 'Largo' in **A** (*Sm*), presumably copied from Handel's addition to copy **B**.

Bar 48 beat 4. Dynamic markings here and in bar 49 do not appear in **B**, and are clearly an addition by Handel to **A**, presumably added in 1738.

Bar 49 soprano. Last note f^2 in **B**, giving consecutive octaves with Alto 2. In **A** it appears that Handel has altered the note from f^2 to d^2.

Bars 52 – 56. At some stage Handel considered cutting these bars and ending the movement with a semibreve at bar 52. Since the movement appears uncut in **B**, this does not apply to Version 1. In **A** Handel wrote 'stat' in pencil next to the deleted bars: I take this to mean that he considered the cut for Version 2, but did not carry it into effect and restored the bars before the performance.

Bar 54. Handel at first wrote 'pianiss' here in

A, but altered this to 'piu pian'. Smith renders it as 'pia pia' in **B**.

No. 3 'larghetto' in **A** and **B** (both *Sm*).

Bar 18 *bc*. Both **A** and **B** have 'soli' here, though Handel equally clearly wrote 'solo' at bars 1 and 5.

No. 4ᴬ Bar 3 'pour' miscopied as 'powr' in **B**.

No. 4ᴮ Bar 7 'andante' in **D**, accidentally omitted by Smith in **A**.

No. 5 No *tempo* mark in **B**. **A** has 'allegro'(*Sm*), deleted in pencil.

Bar 33 beat 3. Tenor has ♭b, viola has a^1, both notes clear in Handel's autograph. At this point he was adding orchestral parts to material from Anthem 6D.

No. 6 'Larghetto' by Handel in **A**, copied by Smith in **B**.

Bars 36, 47 beat 3. Handel's even-note rhythms are clear and presumably deliberate.

Bars 37 – 38 *et seq*. Handel treated 'disquieted' as three syllables in this figure throughout. Later copies of the **N – Q, S** group insert an inauthentic passing note into 'quieted' to produce four syllables.

Bar 43 beat 1, *bc*. The note d^1 is clear in **A** and **B**: *a* is a possible alternative bass note, but does not have any authority from the sources.

Bars 60 – 61. Handel's word-underlay is spread out horizontally in these bars and possibly ambiguous: I have assumed editorially that here as elsewhere he intended 'disquieted' to be treated as three syllables.

Bar 69 beat 3. Tenor rhythm ♫♫ in **A** and **B**: amended to conform to alto. Editorial suggestions for further rhythmic alteration are in conformity with oboe in bar 70: however, a distinction may possibly have been intended by Handel.

Bar 92. Length of final notes in vocal parts shortened editorially from dotted minims.

No. 7 'andante' by Handel in **A**, copied by Smith in **B**.

Bar 88 bass voice. Note shortened editorially from minim.

Some minor editorial readings which affect details of orchestral parts only are noted in the full score included with the hire material for this edition.

The Keyboard Part

The keyboard part of this vocal score is an arrangement derived from the orchestral score. While attempting to convey the essentials of rhythm, harmony and figuration, together with some filling-out of the *basso continuo*, it aims at practical simplicity rather than compressing all musical activity into short score.

The orchestral bass part is transcribed as the lowest line of the accompaniment except in No. 2, where the bass has been transposed up an octave from bar 37 beat 3 to the end of bar 38 for practical reasons. A full realisation of the *basso continuo* part is included with the hire material accompanying this edition, and any anomalous figures from the primary sources are noted there. Handel's 'solo' and 'tutti' annotations from the bass line of the orchestral score are reproduced here. They reflect the density of orchestral and vocal textures and generally indicate the alternation of the continuo group with full orchestral bass scoring. In No. 4ᴮ 'tutti' may have been intended by Handel to denote the entry of bassoons. Any supplementary 'solo' and 'tutti' indications supplied editorially are shown in square brackets.

Certain modifications to the scoring of the bass line were shown by Handel by the use of more than one stave, or by changes of clef. Reductions to the continuo group only, but within 'Tutti' contexts, are indicated editorially by '*Cont.*', with '*Bassi*' for the re-entry of the full bass group. These have been added as a guide to the absence or presence of 16′ orchestral tone. Two special cases need further elucidation:

No. 1 At the beginning of this movement Handel employed two bass staves, labelled 'Violonc' and 'Org et B' respectively. At the end of bar 1, and parallel places later in the movement marked *Vc*, the second stave has rests and presumably double basses and organ continuo are silenced.

No. 7 Bars 3 – 13. Handel's (unlabelled) continuo bass is given in the keyboard reduction: on another stave in the score he gives a skeletal orchestral bass part for these bars in the same rhythm as the upper strings.

Acknowledgements

I am grateful to the owners and keepers of the sources on which this edition is based for access to the material in their collections, and to Watkins Shaw for his assistance with the presentation of this edition.

DONALD BURROWS
1988

1 Versions of the anthem are referred to by the designations given by Friedrich Chrysander in the *Händelgesellschaft* edition (Vols. 34, 36). For a more detailed account of the relationship of the various versions see my article, 'Handel's "As Pants the Hart" ', *The Musical Times*, cxxvi (1985), 113.

2 See Martin Picker, 'Handeliana in the Rutgers University Library', *Journal of the Rutgers University Library*, xxix (1965), 1.

DURATION
ABOUT 16 MINUTES (VERSION 1)
ABOUT 23 MINUTES (VERSION 2)

INSTRUMENTATION

Oboe, Bassoon *ad lib*, Strings, Continuo (Organ).
Version 2 requires 2 Oboes, and Harpsichord may be used for Continuo.

Full score and instrumental material,
including a realised continuo part,
are available on hire.

It is requested that on all concert notices and programmes
reference should be made to Burrows' edition (Novello & Company Limited).

AS PANTS THE HART

Edited by Donald Burrows

G.F. HANDEL

1. Sinfonia

Either Version A :

49

Segue No. 2 (p.**7**)

Or Version B :

adagio

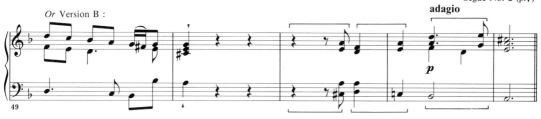

49

p

(Segue allegro)

Allegro
Vlns.

Vlns., Obs.

[*f*]

54

58

[Tutti]

62

66

(Segue No. 2)

2. As pants the hart

Soli and Chorus

1)The alternative editorial distribution shown in brackets enables the movement to be performed with four soloists SATB.

8

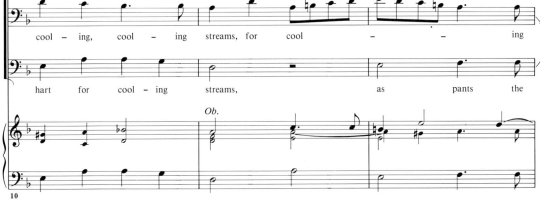

1) The alternative editorial distribution shown in brackets enables the movement to be performed with four soloists SATB.

2)bars 18 and 20. See preface.

12

37

40

3) bar 37. See preface.

43

[Cont.]   [Bassi]

46

4) bars 48-9. Dynamics to all voices and instruments are Handel's,
   but apply to Version 2 only. For Version 1, maintain *forte* throughout.

3. Tears are my daily food
Alto Solo

food, my dai – ly—— food when thus they say,

when thus, when thus—— they say: where is now thy God? where is now thy

[Tutti]

God? where is now thy God? where,——— where is

now thy God? Tears, tears, tears———

[Solo]

are ____ my dai - ly food, tears _____ are my __ dai - ly food

when thus they say, when thus they say: where is now thy

God? where is now thy God? where, where,

where is __ now thy God? where, where is now thy God?

Segue Version 1 No. 4ᴬ
Segue Version 2 No. 4ᴮ

4ᴬ. Now, when I think thereupon

Bass Solo

Segue No. 5 (p. 23)
Tempo **Allegro**

4ᴮ. Now, when I think thereupon

Bass Solo and Chorus

and _____ brought them

out in – to the house of

God, _____

for I went with the

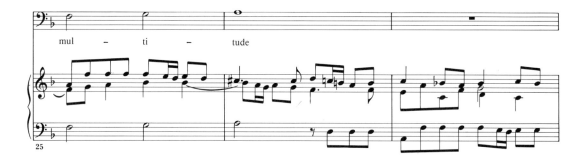

mul – ti – tude

25

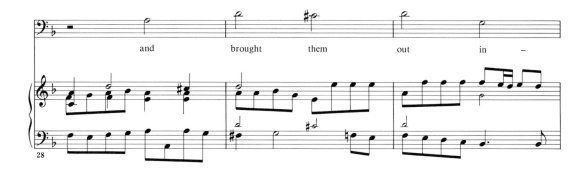

and brought them out in –

28

to the house of God.

31

34

Segue No. 5
Tempo **Andante**
(l'istesso tempo)

5. In the voice of praise

Chorus

as keep ho-ly-day, a-mong such as keep ho-ly-day, a-mong such as keep ho –

ho-ly-day, a-mong such as keep ho – – – ly –

ho-ly-day, a-mong such as keep ho – ly-day, as keep ho – ly –

day, a-mong such as keep ho-ly-day, a-mong such as keep ho – ly-day.

18

– ly – day.

day, a-mong such as keep ho-ly-day,

day, a-mong such as keep ho-ly –

In the voice of praise, of thanks-giv – ing, a-mong such as keep ho-ly-day.

21

[*Cont.*]

praise, in the voice of praise, of thanks-giv – ing, in the voice of praise, of thanks-

day, a-mong such as keep ho – ly - day,

in the voice of praise, of thanks-giv – ing, a-mong such as keep ho - ly - day,—— ho - ly -

giv - ing, of thanks-giv – ing, in the voice of praise, of thanks-giv – ing,

30

adagio

giv – ing, a-mong such as keep ho – ly – day.

a-mong such as keep ho-ly – day, as keep ho – ly – day.

day, as keep ho – ly – day, as keep ho – ly – day.

a-mong such as keep ho-ly – day, as keep ho – ly – day.

adagio

33

6. Why so full of grief, O my soul?

Duet

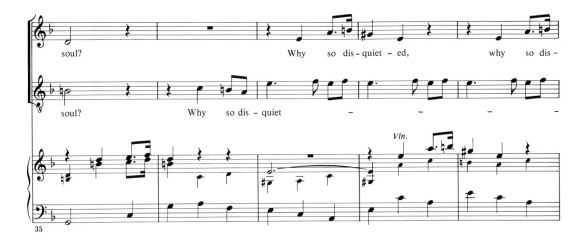

why so dis-quiet-ed, why, _____ why? _____

50

- ed? Why so full of grief, why

Why so full of grief, _____ why

55

so dis-quiet - ed with - in me?

so dis-quiet - ed with - in me? Why so full of

Ob., Vln.

Ob.

60

1) bar 79, basso continuo. See Preface.

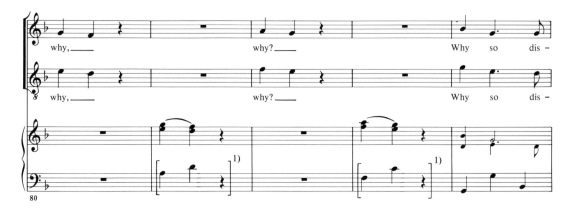

[*attacca* No. 7]

1) Bars 81, 83, basso continuo. See Preface.

7. Put thy trust in God

Bass Solo and Chorus

1) bar 3, basso continuo. See Preface.

29

32

Either Version A

Adagio

praise him,   for   I   will   praise_____ him.

praise him,   for   I   will   praise   him.

praise him,   for   I   will   praise   him.

praise him,   for   I   will   praise   him.

Adagio

40

[Version A ends here]

Or Version B

praise him;   Al – le – lu – ja,_____   al – le – lu –

praise him;   Al – le – lu – ja,_____   al – le   –   lu –

praise him;   Al – le – lu – ja, al – le – lu – ja,

praise him;

[*f*]

40

ja, ... al – le – lu – ja, al –

ja, al – le – lu – ja, al – le – lu – ja, ... al – le –

al – le – lu – ja, al – le – lu – ja, al – le – lu – ja, al –

Al – le – lu – ja, _____ al – le – lu – ja,

43

[Cont.]

le – lu – ja, al – le – lu – ja, al – le – lu – ja, al – le – lu – ja, al –

– lu – ja, al – le – lu – ja, al – le – lu –

le – lu – ja, al – le – lu – ja, al – le – lu – ja,

al – le – lu – ja, al – le – lu – ja, al – le – lu – ja, al –

46

[Bassi.]

le - lu - ja, al - le - lu - ja, al - le - lu - ja, al - le - lu - ja, al - le - lu -

ja, al - le - lu - ja,_____ al - le - lu - ja, al - le - lu -

al - le - lu - ja,_____ al - le - lu -

le - lu - ja,_____ al - le - lu - ja,

49

[Cont.]

ja, al - le - lu - ja,_____ al - le - lu - ja,

ja, al - le - lu - ja, al - le - lu - ja,_____

ja, al - le - lu - ja,_____ al - le - lu - ja,

al -

52

[Bassi]

al – le – lu – ja, al – le – lu – ja, al – le – lu – ja, al – le – lu –

al – le – lu – ja, al – le – lu – ja, al – le – lu – ja, al – le – lu –

al – le – lu – ja, al – le – lu – ja, al – le – lu – ja, al – le – lu –

le – lu – ja, al – le – lu – ja,

55

[Cont.]

ja, al – le – lu – ja, al – le – lu – ja, al – le – lu –

ja, al – le – lu – ja, al – le – lu – ja,

ja, al – le – lu – ja,

58

85

88

ja, al – le-lu – ja, al – le – lu-ja, al – le – lu – ja,

ja,_____ al – le – lu – ja,__ al – le – lu – ja,

al-le-lu – ja,_____ al – le – lu – ja,__

_____ al – le – lu – ja, al – le – lu – ja, al –

97

al – le-lu – ja,_____ al – le – lu – ja,_____ [al –

al – le – lu – ja,_____ [al –

_ al – le – lu – ja,__

le – lu – ja,_____ al – le – lu – ja,_____ al –

100

Printed and bound in Great Britain by
Caligraving Limited Thetford Norfolk